Note to Parents and Teachers

The READING ABOUT: STARTERS series introduces key science vocabulary and concepts to young children while encouraging them to discover and understand the world around them. The series works as a set of graded readers in three levels.

LEVEL 3: READ ALONE follows guidelines set out in the National Curriculum for Year 3 in schools. These books can be read alone or as part of guided or group reading. Each book has three sections:

• Information pages that introduce key concepts. Key words appear in bold for easy recognition on pages where the related science concepts are explained.
• A lively story that recalls this vocabulary and encourages children to use these words when they talk and write.
• A quiz asks children to look back and recall what they have read.

LOOKING AFTER MYSELF looks at HEALTH and DIET. Below are some answers and activities related to the questions on the information spreads that parents, carers and teachers can use to discuss and develop further ideas and concepts:

p. 6 *What is your body telling you when you feel thirsty?* You need water! A 7-8 year-old should drink around seven glasses of water each day and especially after exercise.

p. 11 *Which muscles feel like they have been working hard after making a bed?*
The arm muscles will probably feel tired, along with back muscles from bending over.

p. 13 *Do you feel your heart and lungs working harder after exercise?* Encourage children to run around playground then feel their faster pulse and breathing. Explain that when we work our body hard our lungs and heart can't keep up so we get out of breath.

p. 17 *Why do you think skin that is hidden under your clothes is paler than the rest of your skin?* Skin hidden from the Sun doesn't get tanned like exposed skin.

p. 17 *Why do you need to wear sunglasses when the Sun is very bright?* Explain that sunglasses protect our eyes from harmful (UV) rays. Wrap-around sunglasses also protect the tender skin around our eyes.

p. 19 *Why shouldn't you eat food you have dropped on the floor?* The floor is covered in germs that we can't see. Remind children to always wash their hands before eating.

p. 21 *How does rotting fruit look or smell?* If food doesn't look mouldy or smell bad, then the taste will often tell us if it is going bad. If in doubt, don't eat it!

p. 23 *Why do you think holidays are important?* Holidays give our bodies a chance to rest. They also allow us to relax and to have fun with family and friends.

ADVISORY TEAM

Educational Consultant
Andrea Bright – Science Co-ordinator, Trafalgar Junior School, Twickenham

Literacy Consultant
Jackie Holderness – former Senior Lecturer in Primary Education, Westminster Institute, Oxford Brookes University

Series Consultants
Anne Fussell – Early Years Teacher and University Tutor, Westminster Institute, Oxford Brookes University

David Fussell – C.Chem., FRSC

CONTENTS

© Aladdin Books Ltd 2005

Designed and produced by
Aladdin Books Ltd
2/3 Fitzroy Mews
London W1T 6DF

First published in
Great Britain in 2005 by
Franklin Watts
96 Leonard Street
London EC2A 4XD

A catalogue record for this
book is available from the
British Library.

ISBN 0 7496 6250 6 (H'bk)
ISBN 0 7496 6383 9 (P'bk)
Printed in Malaysia

All rights reserved

Editor: Jim Pipe
Design: Flick, Book Design
and Graphics
Thanks to:
• The pupils of Trafalgar Junior
School, Twickenham and St.
Paul's C.E. Primary School,
Addlestone, for appearing as
models in this book.
• Andrea Bright, Janice Bibby
and Stephanie Cox for helping to
organise the photoshoots.
• The pupils and teachers of
Trafalgar Junior School,
Twickenham and St. Nicholas
C.E. Infant School, Wallingford,
for testing the sample books.

Photocredits:
l-left, r-right, b-bottom, t-top,
c-centre, m-middle
Cover tl, 15mr — Brand X Pictures.
Cover tm & tr, 5br, 7br, 8ml,
14bl, 18br — Corbis. Cover main,
16tr, 19tl, 22m — Comstock.
2tr, 2br, 4tl, 9 both, 18tr, 20mr,
22bl, 23 — Iconotec.com. 2mr,
15bl, 23b — TongRo. 3, 4b, 5tr,
12, 13bl, 16b, 17br, 31tr, 31br —
Photodisc. 5tl, 6ml, 20b — DAJ.
5bl, 11ml, 21br, 31bcr — Jim Pipe.
6br, 10br, 13tr, 20tl, 24tr, 25 all,
26mr, 27 all, 28-29 all, 30 both,
31ml, 31bcl — Marc Arundale/
Select Pictures. 7m, 21t — USDA.
8mr, 26ml, 31br — Stockbyte.
10tl, 14mr, 17tr & m, 22tr —
Digital Vision. 15t — Corel.
19mr & bl — PBD. 25bl —
Ingram Publishing.

Starters

Looking
After Myself

by Sally Hewitt

Aladdin/Watts
London • Sydney

A HEALTHY BODY

You have an amazing **body**.
But you need to look after
it so that it stays strong
and **healthy**.

Your **body** needs fresh air
and exercise, good food,
plenty of water and rest
and sleep.

You can help to keep your brain **healthy**
by giving yourself lots of interesting
things to think about.

Using your brain

Here are some other things that keep your **body** and brain **healthy**.

Learning
Learning something new, reading, music and playing games are all good for your brain.

Having fun
Being happy helps to keep you healthy. Good friends or a pet to love can make you feel happy.

Keeping clean
As well as washing your body, you need to clean your teeth every day.

Visiting a doctor
It's good to go to the doctor and dentist for a regular check-up.

FOOD AND ENERGY

Every day, your amazing body builds itself and grows. It uses lots of **energy**. It fights germs and heals when you have been hurt.

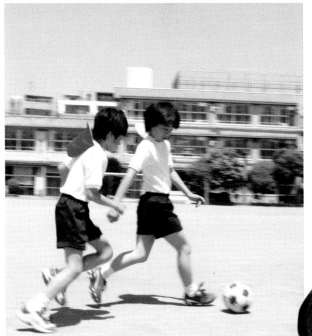

To be able to do all these things, your body needs **food**.

Using energy

When you feel hungry, your body is telling you it needs food.

What is it telling you when you feel thirsty?

Eat lots of fruit and vegetables.
They are full of vitamins and minerals.

Bread, pasta and all kinds of cereals give you
energy. These **foods** are called carbohydrates.

A healthy meal

Meat, fish, cheese and
nuts contain proteins.
These **foods** help your
body to build and grow.

What types of **food** can
you see in the meal above?

You need some
sugar, salt and fat
every day.

But too many fatty
or sweet foods are
bad for your health.

7

LOOKING AFTER YOUR TEETH

Strong **teeth** are important for keeping healthy. You chew your food with them and they give you a nice smile!

Animals that eat meat have pointed **teeth** for tearing. Animals that eat plants have flat **teeth** for chewing.

Pointed teeth

Flat teeth

Look at your teeth in the mirror.

• Find your sharp front teeth, called incisors, for biting.
• Your pointed side teeth, called canines, are for tearing.
• Your flat back teeth, called molars, are for chewing.

Incisors

Canines

Molars

Look after your **teeth**.
It's hard to eat without them!

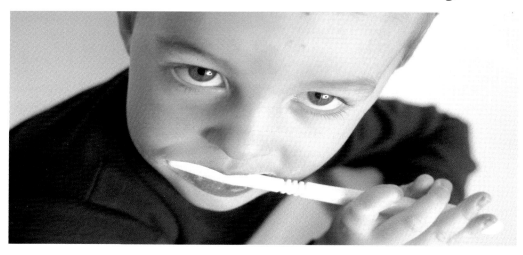

Clean your **teeth** every morning and
night to get rid of little bits of
food and germs. If they are left
on your **teeth**, they cause tooth decay.

Brush all your **teeth** carefully.
Rinse your mouth out with water.

Tooth decay is when
your teeth go bad.

Too many sweet foods
or drinks can make
your teeth decay.

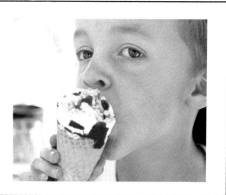

9

BONES AND MUSCLES

Your body is supported by your skeleton. This is made up of 206 **bones**.

Running, walking and jumping keep your **bones** strong. The minerals in foods such as fish, nuts and milk help to build strong **bones** too.

Skeleton

Straight

Slouched

Your posture is how you stand. A straight posture helps your bones to support your body.

Under your skin are about 650 **muscles**. Big **muscles** in your back, legs and arms pull your **bones** when you move. **Muscles** inside you work your heart and stomach.

Muscles

When you move, you work your **muscles**. The harder you make your **muscles** work, the stronger they get.

Make your bed. Fluff up the pillows. Shake out the duvet. Tuck in the sheets.

Which muscles feel like they have been working hard?

11

Breathing in

LUNGS AND HEART

Every part of your body needs
oxygen from the air.
You breathe air through
your mouth and nose
and down to your **lungs**.

Your **lungs** are like two
big sponges. But instead
of soaking up water,
they soak up air.

Lungs

Sit still. Find your pulse and feel your heartbeat. Put your hand on your chest and feel yourself breathing in and out.

Now do some exercise. Do you feel your heart and lungs working harder?

Oxygen from the air goes into your blood. Your **heart** pumps blood full of oxygen round and round your body through tubes called blood vessels.

Running and dancing are the kinds of exercise that work your heart and lungs and keep them healthy.

Heart

13

EXERCISE

Exercise makes your body work hard.
It helps to keep you fit and healthy.
You can do all kinds of different **exercise**.

Bike riding, skating and skateboarding
are fun. Wear a helmet, knee
and elbow pads in case you
have a fall!

Skateboarding

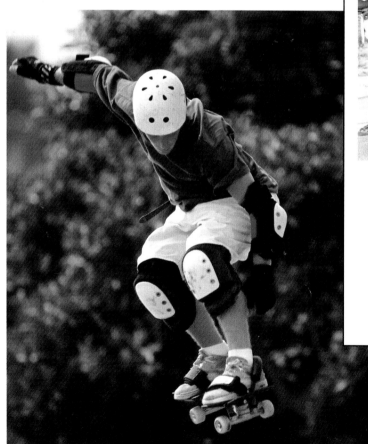

You need to
learn how to
cycle safely
on roads and
cycle paths.

Team games

Everyone works hard together in team games.

You train to get fitter and to practise skills. Spectators come to watch you play and cheer when you score!

Walking to school, playing in the park and making your bed are all kinds of exercise.

What exercise do you do every day? What new exercise would you like to do?

SUNSHINE AND FRESH AIR

It feels good to go outside, breathe **fresh air** and feel the **sunshine** on your skin.

Your skin uses **sunlight** to make vitamin D which helps to make your bones strong. But too much **Sun** can burn your skin.

In the Sun

A sunhat and sun cream can help to protect your skin from the hot Sun.

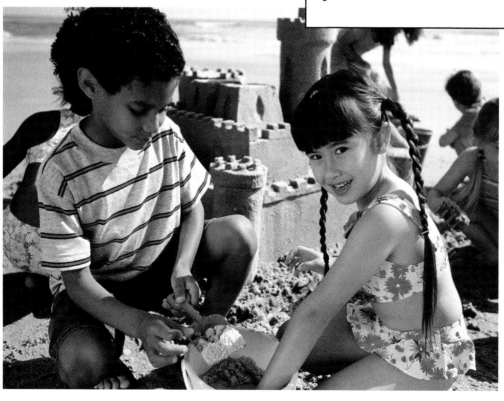

Smoke from chimneys, traffic and cigarettes make the **air** dirty. It's better not to breathe in too much dirty **air**!

Trees help to keep the **air** clean. The park, the countryside and the seaside are good places to enjoy the **fresh air**.

Fresh air

Why do you think skin that is hidden under your clothes is paler than the rest of your skin?

Why do you need to wear sunglasses when the Sun is very bright?

KEEPING CLEAN

Every day, your hair, skin and nails get dirty. Your skin gets hot and sweaty.

If you don't wash, the sweat and dirt on your body soon gets smelly.

You need to have a bath or shower, **clean** your nails and wash your hair to smell **clean**!

Many animals spend lots of time keeping clean.

This rhinoceros is taking a mud bath to clean bugs off its skin!

18

Paws and feet walk over the floor.

Why shouldn't you eat food you have dropped on the floor?

Washing our skin keeps it healthy. Dirty skin can become sore.

Tiny germs can get into cuts on your skin.

Getting dirty

Your clothes need a wash. They get smelly and dirty too!

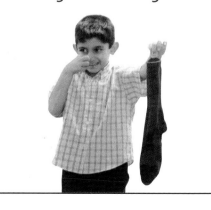

Germs in dirt on your hands can make you ill.

Wash your hands after you have been to the toilet and if you have touched soil.

19

FIGHTING GERMS

Germs that give you coughs and colds fly through the air when you cough and sneeze. Use a hanky so no one else catches them!

Resting and keeping warm when you are ill helps your body to **fight germs** and get better.

Resting

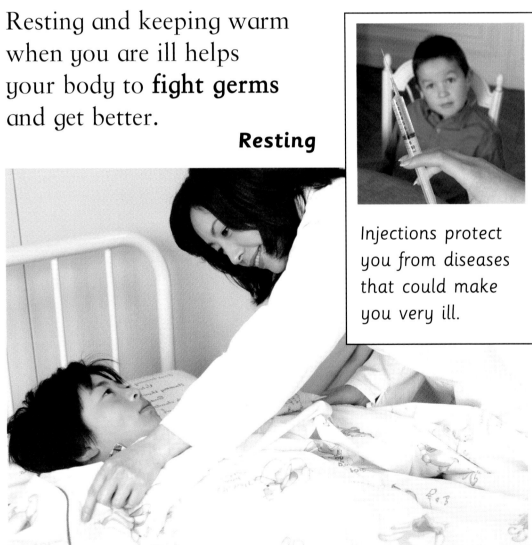

Injections protect you from diseases that could make you very ill.

A clean kitchen

People who prepare food keep the kitchen very clean. They wash their hands before they touch food. A hat holds back their hair.

Fruit and vegetables are washed.
Fresh food is stored in a refrigerator.

Germs on food start to make it rot when it gets old.

Our senses can help to warn us. How does rotting fruit look or smell?

Rotting fruit

CHANGE AND REST

Your body works hard all day. It is important to have a **change** and a **rest**.

A drink of water helps your body to work better whatever you are doing.

When you are reading, writing or working on the computer, take a break and have a good stretch.

Sleeping

Sleep is an important part of keeping healthy. Imagine how tired your body would get if you never went to sleep!

While you are asleep, your body keeps working. Your brain is still thinking. Your heart keeps beating and you keep breathing, but everything slows down.

Weekends and holidays give you a break from school. Why do you think they are important? What activities do you like to do on holiday?

23

I FEEL ILL!

Look out for words about your body and keeping healthy.

Mia sneezed very loudly three times. "Oh dear," said Mum. "Have you got a cold?" Mia sneezed again.

"Use your hanky!" said Ronnie. "I don't want to catch your germs."

Mum put Mia to bed.
"It's not bedtime!" she cried.
But as soon as she curled up
under the duvet, she fell asleep.
Mum and Ronnie tip-toed out of the room.

Mia stayed in bed all the next day. Ronnie started to play a computer game in his bedroom next door.

"Sshh! Not too loud," said Mum. "Mia needs peace and quiet!"

The day after that, Mia felt a bit better.
"I'm bored!" she said.
"I want to go outside
and play!"

"Tomorrow," said Mum.
Mia was very cross and
grumpy. She didn't want
to stay in bed.

Ronnie read Mia a story.
He played cards with her.
He put on a puppet show.

Mia laughed and clapped.

"Thank you for
cheering Mia up,"
Mum said to Ronnie.
"You've helped her
to feel much better."

The next day was warm and sunny.
"You can go outside today," said Mum.
"But first, eat your breakfast."

Mia was hungry.
She had a bowl of
porridge, orange
juice and a banana.

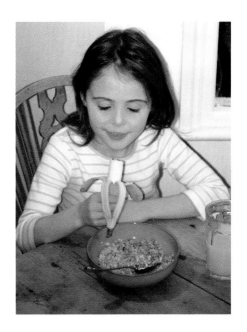

"That will build
your strength up!"
said Mum.

"I need lots of strength too!" said Ronnie.

"I'm playing in the school
basketball team on Saturday."

After breakfast, they walked
to the park. Mia skipped
with her rope. Ronnie
practised with his basketball.
Mum threw a ball
for Pluto the dog.

Mum gave them all
a drink of water.
"Don't forget Pluto,"
said Mia.

Mia said, "I'm tired!"
"That's because you've been ill,"
said Mum. "We can come again tomorrow.
You'll feel a bit stronger every day."

"You'll soon have strong muscles
like me!" said Ronnie.
"Exercise helps to give us strong
muscles and bones. It gives
us energy too," said Mum.

Mia threw the ball and
        Pluto chased after it.
            "Energy like
            Pluto?"
            asked Mia.
            "Just like Pluto,"
            said Mum.

When they got home, Mia had a rest
while Mum and Ronnie made the beds.

"Making the beds is hard
work!" said Ronnie. "I can
feel my heart beating fast."
"Housework is good exercise.
It keeps you fit!" said Mum.

"Will it keep me fit for the
match?" said Ronnie.
Mum laughed. "It will help," she said.

Mia got up. "I'll sweep the floor," said Ronnie.
"Then I'll lay the table. Come and help, Mia!"

"I'll help tomorrow,
when I'm better,"
said Mia.

At bedtime, Mia said,
"I'm too tired to clean
my teeth!"

"You'll get tooth decay!" joked Ronnie.
"You need to clean your teeth twice a day!"

Ronnie cleaned his teeth carefully, rinsed his mouth with water and smiled at the mirror. His teeth were white and strong.

"I don't want tooth decay!"
said Mia. So she cleaned her
teeth and smiled at the mirror.
Her teeth were white and strong too.

Mum tucked them up in bed and kissed them both goodnight.

"I want to be in a basketball
team like Ronnie,"
said Mia.

"I'll teach you to play tomorrow," said Ronnie.

The next day, they went to the park to practise. Mia was full of energy.

"Basketball is fun!" said Mia. "You'll have to train hard," said Ronnie. "And eat lots of good food!" said Mum.

"No problem!" grinned Mia. "I feel like I could join the team today!"

WRITE YOUR OWN STORY about keeping healthy. Make a chart like this to see if the things you do most days can help to keep you fit and healthy.

	Eating	Reading	Sleeping	Football	Washing
Gives me energy	✔				
Makes me strong	✔			✔	
Makes me think		✔			
Fights germs	✔		✔		✔
Gives me a rest			✔		

QUIZ

You think with your brain. What can you do to keep your brain **healthy**?

Answer on pages 4 and 5

Bones support your body. What helps to keep them strong?

Answer on pages 10 and 11

Germs can make you ill. What can you do to fight **germs**?

Answer on pages 20 and 21

What parts of your body do these things?

Pump blood around your body

Move your bones

Breathe

Chew

Answers on pages 8, 11, 12, 13

INDEX